EROTIC DRAWINGS

First published in the United States of America in 1986 by
Rizzoli International Publications, Inc.
597 Fifth Avenue, New York, N.Y. 10017

Copyright © Phaidon Press Limited, Oxford, 1986

Library of Congress Cataloging in Publication Data

Tilly, Andrew
  Erotic drawings.
  1. Erotic drawing.   I. Tilly, Andrew.
NC825.E76E75   1986   743′.928   85-43477
ISBN 0-8478-0696-0 (pbk.)

Printed in Great Britain by Blantyre Printing
and Binding Company Limited, Glasgow

Man and Woman by Pablo Picasso.
1927.
Etching, $7\frac{1}{2} \times 11$ in.

EROTIC DRAWINGS

Andrew Tilly

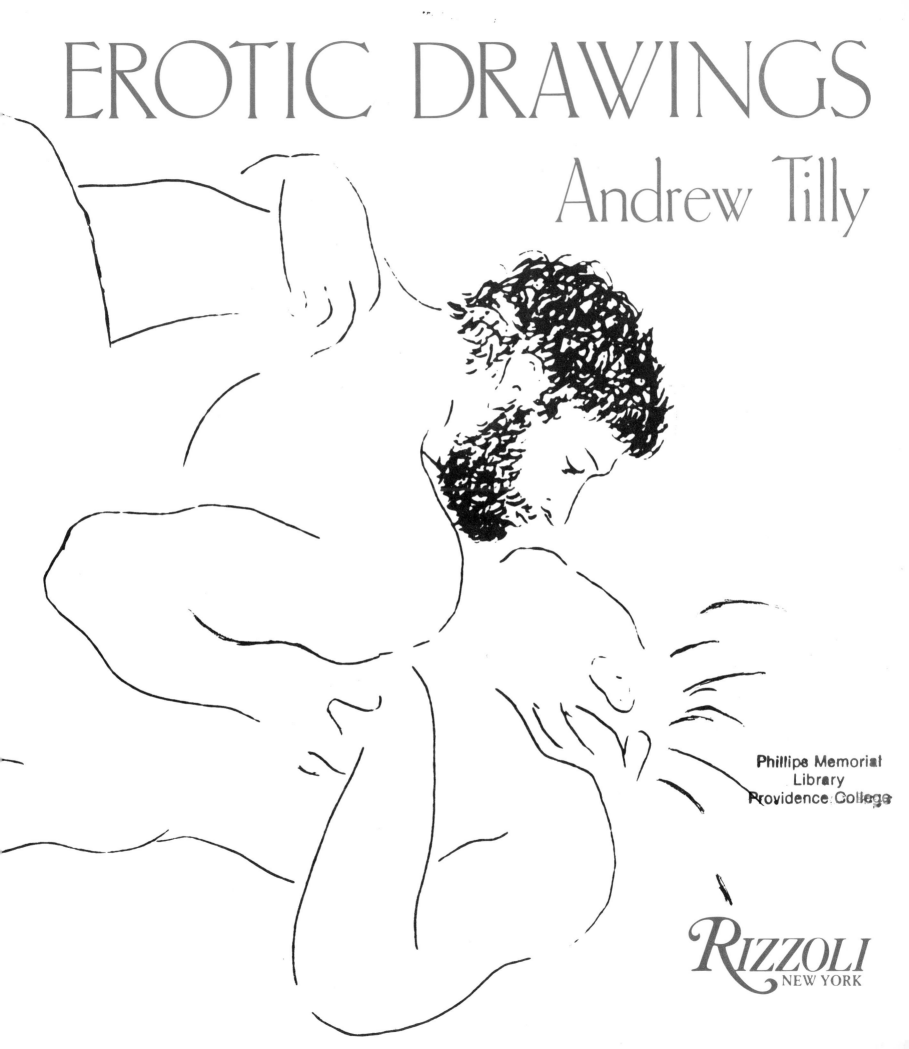

RIZZOLI
NEW YORK

1. Titian (1480/5–1576). *A Couple in Embrace*. *c*.1570. Charcoal and black chalk, heightened with white, on blue paper. 9⅞ × 10¼ in. (25.1 × 26 cm.) Fitzwilliam Museum, Cambridge.

The Western artistic tradition is dominated by the Judaeo-Christian association of sex and guilt. Searching through the art of the past in quest of the erotic imagination, we engage in a version of archaeology, prying behind the surface of art's public, acceptable exterior. In this sense, the drawing occupies a central place in Western erotic art. In their drawings, artists give vein to aspects of the imagination that find no place in their public, finished work. Drawings can be private or experimental; the erotic drawing is the archetypal underground image.

In 1855, Robert Browning published a witty poem on art and the temptations of the flesh. 'Fra Lippo Lippi' is written as a dramatic monologue, in which the great Renaissance artist tells the story of his escape from captivity to an amorous rendezvous with a group of nuns. Cosimo de Medici had locked Lippi away to ensure that he completed one of his commissions—'A-painting for the great man, saints and saints/And saints again . . .' We meet him creeping back to bed after a night of lecherous revelry, 'Ere I rise up to-morrow and go work/On Jerome knocking at his poor old breast/With his great round stone to subdue the flesh'. Browning's poem is an amusing comment on the subversive relation of *eros* to art. In the Renaissance, when the artist was meant to be the moral and spiritual guide of man, sexuality was a subterranean force, driven underground by the artistic ideology of the time. Browning's Lippi comically embodies the rebellion of the flesh—his imprisonment in the service of art becomes, quite literally, a metaphor for Renaissance art's imprisonment of the body in the service of the spirit.

Few genuinely erotic Renaissance drawings survive. If we turn from Browning's frustrated Lippi to the wonderful High Renaissance drawing *The Rape of Ganymede* (by or after Michelangelo), we find an image that underlines the problematic role of eroticism in Renaissance art (Fig. 2). On one level, the drawing is a vision of erotic ecstasy—Ganymede surrenders his gorgeously modelled anatomy to the embrace of Jupiter, who has transformed himself into an eagle. Some art historians attribute the drawing to Michelangelo, and at one time this was believed to be the drawing which the artist gave to Tommaso de' Cavalieri in 1532. Michelangelo was infatuated by Cavalieri, and in a typically twentieth-century interpretation, *The Rape of Ganymede* becomes a confessional work, a love-token. The interpretation is reinforced when we recall that the iconography of this myth found favour with artists in ancient Greece because it seemed to offer religious sanction for homosexual relationships. It is tempting to read the drawing as a private

2. Anon, after Michelangelo (16th century). *The Rape of Ganymede*. 1532 or after. Black chalk and pen. $7\frac{1}{2} \times 10\frac{1}{4}$ in. (19 × 26 cm.) Royal Collection, Windsor Castle.

epistle, but not entirely accurate. The immortal Jupiter had fallen in love with the mortal Ganymede and borne him off to Olympus; over centuries of subsequent Christian interpretation, the myth had operated as an allegory of religious redemption. In the mediaeval *Moralised Ovid*, Ganymede and Jupiter became prefigurations of St John the Evangelist and Christ; for Renaissance humanists, the story allegorized the human soul's progress to God. In this light Ganymede's triumphant ascent, his idealized anatomy, and his sexual congress with Jupiter act as symbols of spiritual purity. If the drawing is erotic, its eroticism remains ambiguous—the physical is displaced by the spiritual, *eros* mingled with spiritual allusions. Michelangelo may be expressing his love for Cavalieri, but on a Platonic level.

Eros in Renaissance art is nearly always dignified or dissipated as allegory. Venetian art often seems more secular than its Roman or Florentine counterparts—in the work of Titian, myth seems less insistent in its demands on nudity to *mean* something. His mythological paintings are strewn with courtesans posing as Venuses, while his drawing, *A Couple in Embrace*, is a study in the voluptuous handling of form (Fig. 1). Where Michelangelo uses line to indicate purity, a weightless anatomy of the spirit, Titian's massed lines and heavy shading suggest the heaviness of flesh. Titian's graphic technique, which emphasizes the solidity and presence of his figures, is equivalent to the way he handles paint. But whereas in a painting these lovers would be given mythological status (as *Mars and Venus*, most probably), the informal, private nature of a sketch points to the straightforward eroticism of Titian's art. Lacking a title, Titian's drawing comes still closer to twentieth-century erotic sensibilities than his more finished, public work.

For the most part, the bizarre erotic fantasies of the Italian Mannerists survive only in engravings—Giulio Romano's or Marcantonio Raimondi's illustrations to Aretino's lewd stories, or Parmigianino's weird, occult *Witches' Sabbath* (Fig. 3). The erotic drawings that have been selected for reproduction in the main section of this book all date from the eighteenth century onwards. The eighteenth century witnesses the collapse of a tradition in which *eros* is suppressed by myth; Fragonard, for example, may still disguise his erotic fantasy, *The Sacrifice of the Rose* (Plate 2), as spurious allegory, but the disguise is so thin that it turns into a joke. Elsewhere, Fragonard invents his own, demythologized excuses for eroticism—fire in the bedroom is a favourite (Fig. 4). By the 1820s, when Rowlandson produced his extraordinary hand-tinted engraving *Susannah and the Elders*, classical myth or biblical legend have lost all credibility as masks for eroticism (Fig. 5).

Rowlandson's work operates on several levels—as pornography, and as parody of 'respectable' pornography, a comment on the specious connoisseurship of the eighteenth- and nineteenth-century erotomane. Rowlandson's scene is set in contemporary England; this is a thoroughly modern *Susannah and the Elders*, stripped bare (in every sense) of the decencies usually accorded the myth from which it takes its title. In the biblical story, Susannah was the wife of a prosperous Jew, the victim of a plot by two elders of the community who planned to ravish her. The plot failed and Daniel, the hero of the story, revealed their villainy in court by eliciting conflicting testimony from the two elders. While mediaeval artists avoided the erotic potential of the subject and chose the theme of Daniel instituting justice, Renaissance artists illustrated the elders spying on Susannah as she bathed—a good excuse for the portrayal of female nudity. Rowlandson parodies this convention, crudely pointing to the hypocrisy of the stratagem. He appropriates the story, and absorbs it into his personal mythology of erotic contrast—between the young and sexually vital girl, and the dessicated antiquarian observers who have substituted voyeurism for action. By invoking the mythological eroticism of the past at the same time as he so obviously flouts its proprieties, Rowlandson announces the death of a tradi-

3. Parmigianino (1503–40). *Witches' Sabbath*. 1530s. Etching, 5¾ × 3¾ in. (14.5 × 9.5 cm.) British Museum, London.

tion. From now on, subjects like Diana at her Bath, the Rape of Europa and equivalent erotic sublimations enjoy a fading status in Western art. They certainly survive, in the long, bleak period of kitsch academy erotica that flourished during the nineteenth century and beyond; but the Renaissance language of myth has been debased by the obviousness of such pictures.

This is not to say that overt eroticism became any more socially acceptable in the light of Rowlandson's scurrilous parodies. Far from it. Rowlandson's engraving was one of a series of quasi-pornographic works he produced in his later years. His work would have been privately circulated, testifying to a version of public censorship that continues to the present day. Drawing is perhaps the most potentially subversive (because most private) of art's media—even an artist as obsessed with sexuality as Rowlandson mutes

4. Jean-Honoré Fragonard (1732–1806). *The Jets of Water*. 1770s. Wash, 10¼ × 15 in. (26 × 38 cm.) Sterling and Francine Clark Institute, Williamstown, Mass.

5. Thomas Rowlandson (1756–1827). *Susannah and the Elders*. 1820s. Hand-tinted engraving, 7½ × 7 in. (19 × 17.8 cm.) Victoria and Albert Museum, London.

6. Tomi Ungerer. Cartoon from *Testament*. 1985.

the erotic content of his more public work. *The Statuary's Yard* (Plate 6) is a fine example of Rowlandson's jocose public eroticism; a commentary on voyeurism itself rather than an unveiling of real sexual activity.

Erotic art, as Tomi Ungerer's witty cartoon implies, is often a vehicle for the expression of unhealthy fetishes, revealing the artist as much as his subject (Fig. 6). The history of erotic art is littered with recantations and busily destructive executors tidying up the reputations of dead artists. After Turner's death, Ruskin exhibited his own sense of decency. He personally destroyed several sheets of erotic drawings by Turner—though not all, as the one illustrated here demonstrates (Fig. 7). Aubrey Beardsley illustrated Aristophanes' lewd comedy *Lysistrata* in 1896 for a limited edition of the play printed by Leonard Smithers, a man Oscar Wilde described as 'the most learned erotomaniac in Europe' (Plate 13). Just two years later, as he lay dying in Menton, Beardsley wrote to Smithers requesting him to 'destroy all copies of the Lysistrata and bad drawings'. This recantation stemmed less from a sense of shamed propriety, perhaps, than from Beardsley's recognition of the confessional nature of his *Lysistrata* illustrations—they reveal his own attitudes to sexuality in ways that had only been suggested in his less overtly erotic work.

Censorship (and self-censorship) is an interesting phenomenon: less as a peculiar social convention in which (for example) breasts might be acceptable, penises and vaginas not, than because it implies an awareness of the dangerous and dark side of sexuality. As Susan Sontag has argued in her fine essay, 'The Pornographic Imagination', human sexuality is 'a highly questionable phenomenon . . . one of the demonic forces in human consciousness'. Sontag draws her examples from literature; the erotic drawing, also, is a

7. J. M. W. Turner (1775–1851). Sheet of erotic drawings. *c.*1820s. Pencil and wash, 10½ × 14½ in. (26.7 × 36.8 cm.) British Museum, London.

potential revealer of sexual obsessions that embrace pain or death, at least in the imagination.

Henry Fuseli takes the private, obsessional nature of the erotic drawing to its limits. Fuseli made his reputation in 1782, when he exhibited his sensational painting *The Nightmare* at the Royal Academy. He portrayed a long-limbed girl, her body clad in an enticingly clinging nightgown, stretched out on a bed; a devilish, grinning incubus crouches on her chest, while the staring head of a horse (the nightmare) appears in the background. The painting later roused Hazlitt to comment that Fuseli was a nightmare on the breast of British art, a sick fantasist whose horrible dreams sabotaged the true moral function of art. But in a sense, Fuseli's painting is just a performance, a shallowly erotic work made up of symbols for the *possibilities* of sexual fantasy. To see the actual workings of Fuseli's imagination, we must turn to his drawings (Plates 4 and 5). It seems ironic that Fuseli eventually became Professor of Painting at the Royal Academy—in his lectures he would spout the neoclassical cliché, claiming that the artist should suppress the quirks of his personality 'to impress one general idea, one great quality of nature or mode of society, some great maxim'. Fuseli's theory is a sham—his drawings are entirely personal, taking sexuality into the dangerous areas of violence and sado-masochism. Some of his most unpleasant drawings feature prostitutes gleefully murdering babies.

Of course, the drawing is not always an obsessive and solipsistic medium. Even when a drawing is essentially a private production, it is not necessarily a vehicle for disturbing revelations—Klimt's erotic work was done primarily for the artist's own satisfaction, and he drew the female nude with affection rather than *angst* (Fig. 8 and Plate 16). Besides, there is a long tradition in Western art which suggests that drawing is implicitly opposed to eroticism or to irrationality—the theory that line is pure, simple, ideal, whereas colour is confused and sensuous. Ingres was the nineteenth-century's great upholder of this doctrine; self-appointed guardian of purity and reason in an age of decadence, he reviled Delacroix for his sensual abandon to colour and screamed 'traitor!' at Paganini for his passionate musical improvisations. Yet coupled with his insistence on the *bonnes doctrines* of classical art, Ingres was an intensely sensual draughtsman (Baudelaire once said that 'his libertinism is serious and convinced'). This accounts for the curious ambiguity of his erotic images (Plate 11). He would no doubt have been appalled by his inclusion in this book.

One important aspect of the drawing's erotic potential derives from our heightened awareness of its making, its frequent nature as sketch, as incomplete or 'unfinished' image. Drawings are often spontaneous where paintings can seem overworked. As far back as 1699, Roger de Piles, the French aesthetic theorist, defined the sketch in terms that are

8. Gustav Klimt (1826–1918). *Woman.* 1907. Engraving, $11 \times 13\frac{3}{4}$ in. (28 × 35 cm.) British Museum, London.

peculiarly appropriate to its erotic impact—'Imagination supplies all the features which are missing or which have been finished, and each person who sees the sketch fills them in according to his own taste.' This distinction suggests the difference, if one can be established, between eroticism and pornography. The drawing necessarily witholds mimetic completion of the image; it establishes a species of dialogue in which both artist and viewer participate in the image's creation. The artist and his own erotic vision are always present, in the marks his hand has made on paper; the spectator has his own part to play in interpreting those marks, translating graphic conventions into representations. The perfect medium for pornography is the colour photograph, because it hints at no such interchange. Photography offers us a much closer approximation to the presence of flesh than drawing can possibly attempt. Pornography aims at an exhaustive suggestion of the body's presence, a direct confrontation between viewer and sex-object. This confrontation is always sabotaged in a drawing, obstructed by a third presence, that of the artist. Paradoxically, the best erotic art is often the least arousing; where the artist is not working for the consumer, but for himself.

Apologists for erotic art generally adopt a cosily liberal attitude in their discussions of the subject. But the most powerful images in erotic art declare the solipsistic nature of the sexual imagination—Fuseli's drawings, or the compulsive outpourings of Géricault, Schiele, Picasso or de Kooning do not lend themselves easily to arguments for the liberating potential of fantasy (Plates 4, 5, 8, 17, 23 and 26). Erotic art does not turn us into happy and healthy members of a thriving sexual commonwealth. Books on erotic art tend to veer between the mock-learned and the dilettantishly sexist. Producing catalogues of naughty bits in art, their authors are also preachers, inventing a unified, liberating 'tradition' where none exists. Sexual fantasy dislocates the artist, removes him from tradition and reminds him of his refractory subjectivity. One cannot talk meaningfully, therefore, about a Western tradition of erotic drawing; kinds of erotic art are as disparate as kinds of human sexuality. It might be possible to write a history of the public erotic image (from Titian's Venuses to the pin-up) but the result would probably be a subsection of the history of pornography. The images in this book have been chosen because they are powerful, amusing, occasionally representative of a type, or simply interesting. If they are unified, it is by their origins in the West, and their production within a male-dominated artistic culture; aside from that, the book's structure is necessarily and appropriately discursive.

1

FRANCOIS BOUCHER (1703–70)

A Sleeping Girl (c. 1745)

Red, black and white chalk on blue
paper
$8\frac{1}{4} \times 12\frac{1}{2}$ in. (22.3 × 31.7 cm.)
Private collection

Rococo eroticism finds its expression in an art that guarantees total sexual availability of the female form. François Boucher, the great French painter and draughtsman, takes the female nudes of Renaissance and Baroque art— Titian, and above all Rubens—and removes them from clear narrative settings. They become unresisting vehicles for the (implicitly male) sexual imagination. This languorous semi-nude is, typically, asleep: sleep ensures her vulnerability to fantasy; she cannot challenge the viewer's gaze and thus she becomes (like nearly all of Boucher's women) an erotically ideal expanse of flesh on which we are invited to inscribe our desires. This particular drawing is possibly a study for the figure of Diana (which it duplicates) in one of five paintings commissioned by Madame de Pompadour for her château at Bellevue. The highly finished state of the drawing suggests that it was probably commissioned as an independent work by one of the many fashionable patrons who clamoured for such pieces—Boucher's delicate draughtsmanship, with its fine hatching and subtle white chalk highlights that conjure the weight and sheen of flesh, was highly prized by his contemporaries. (It still is highly prized—in 1984 the drawing was sold for £75,600, a record for a Boucher drawing.) As so often in Rococo art female clothing—in this case a beautifully rendered and curiously amorphous drapery-cum-dress—exists only to excite by titillating disclosures. Boucher's sleeping girl signals her complicity in the viewer's fantasy by drawing back one of its folds to reveal an expanse of thigh. Boucher deliberately fails to place her in coherent perspectival space; we can imagine a setting as readily as a story for her. Specificity of action or place is anathema to Rococo eroticism, with its emphasis on the free play of the viewer's fantasy. J. B. Michel unconsciously announced the success of Boucher's image when he engraved it and gave it the title 'Le Repos de la Volupté'. This is no Diana, as Michel's abstract noun declares—it it an anonymous vision of female voluptuousness.

2

JEAN-HONORE FRAGONARD
(1732–1806)

The Sacrifice of the Rose (c. 1780)

Wash and watercolour
$16\frac{1}{2} \times 13$ in. (42 × 33 cm)
Private collection

Fragonard was the master with Boucher of Rococo eroticism in eighteenth-century France. Surprisingly, he never established a successful public career (unlike Boucher), but he found a large middle-class market for his work—especially the many erotic drawings and engravings in which he specialized, where strange accidents lead to titillating revelations. A favourite subject was fire in ladies' bedrooms, with its attendant *risqué* chaos.

In the 1780s, Fragonard executed a series of paintings which could be described as erotic allegories. One of these, *The Sacrifice of the Rose*, is duplicated in the lively watercolour reproduced here. Significantly, Fragonard completed this drawing *after* his painting; his clients valued his drawings for their spontaneity and vibrant line and tones. Fragonard understands the essential rule of Rococo *eros*—never be explicit, or you risk bad taste. Here, eroticism is dressed up as quasi-religious allegory—Fragonard's handsome young angel and swooning heroine are mischievously adapted from the traditional protagonists of an Annunciation. The rose's sacrifice is of course a euphemism for lost virginity; the rose is a time-honoured symbol of female pudenda, while the phallic overtones of the angel's fiery torch need no elaboration. Fragonard wittily substitutes erotic for religious revelation. The putti that swarm around his madonna assist her pleasure, simultaneously undressing and propelling her towards her airborne lover. Cupid, installed on his plinth at top left, is the presiding deity of this amorous consummation. Fragonard's erotic art deals in clever displacements—sexual encounter is rendered as allegory, while sexual excitement is sublimated in the technical virtuosity of the image, those fluidly handled clouds of smoke that act as metaphor for orgasm.

3

ANON—FRENCH 18th Century

Samson and Dalilah

Watercolour
$14\frac{1}{4} \times 10\frac{1}{2}$ in. (36.5 × 26.5 cm.)
British Museum

The *Histoire Universelle* is an intriguing album of erotic watercolours in the British Museum. The album consists of sixty-eight images lewdly adapted from mythological or biblical sources. Henry Spencer Ashbee, a nineteenth-century erotomane, attributed the drawings to Charles-Antoine Coypel, one of the leaders of early eighteenth-century academic painting in France, but this seems extremely dubious. The artist's sinuous Rococo anatomies suggest a date closer to the second half of the century.

The watercolour reproduced here is introduced in the album by a neat copperplate inscription in French: 'Samson and Dalilah (this is the true version of Scripture)'. Like Rowlandson's *Susannah and the Elders* (Fig. 5) the image parodies the conventions of gentle mythological or biblical eroticism. The artist's grasp of human anatomy seems limited; this is partly the result of his pornographic intentions, which rotate figures around their genitalia to ensure that we have an unobstructed view of the essentials. The scene is gloomily lit, so that our attention is focussed on his elongated ductile nudes with their unhealthy sheen. The story of Samson and Dalilah turns into a classic version of castration anxiety in this, the 'true' story. Samson's erect penis is threatened by Dalilah's snipping scissors, ultimate symbol of the *vagina dentata*, as the curls of his pubic hair are cropped. By no means great art, this watercolour is still an interesting (if unpleasant) counterpart to the polite eroticism of Boucher or Fragonard.

4

HENRY FUSELI (1741–1825)

Erotic Scene—Three Women and a Man (1809/10)

Pencil and wash $7\frac{1}{8} \times 9\frac{5}{8}$ in (18 × 24.5 cm.)

Victoria and Albert Museum, London

Fuseli's brooding, obsessional art was entirely circumscribed by his fears and anxieties. His erotic drawings, produced for his own satisfaction rather than for public exhibition, simply crystallize the sexual tensions that lurk in his academic works. The straining, prostrate figure who has been overwhelmed by these three malevolent harpies is the archetypal Fuselian male. For his exhibitable versions of this masochistic theme Fuseli would scour classical mythology, the Bible, ancient and modern literature, as if seeking to disclaim his fantasies by presenting them as 'illustrations' of venerable sources: Brunhild watching Gunther suspended from the ceiling (from the *Niebelunglied*), Margaret mocking York (from Shakespeare's *Henry VI*), or Dalila gloating over the blind Samson, were some of the disguises Fuseli found for his masochism. Even the drawing reproduced here, which takes Fuseli's vision to the intense level of pornography by eschewing such narrative alibis, is apologetically inscribed with a classical reference. The Greek quotation in the bottom right comes from Sophocles' *Prometheus*: 'in such a way may love come upon my enemies', which refers to an account of wives murdering their husbands on their wedding night. Fuseli's drawing is an image of emasculation. His muscly women, with their massive haunches, derive from the masculine female nudes of Michelangelo (Fuseli's artistic hero), while their ornate, phallically tumescent coiffures underline their confiscation of the man's sexual initiative; potency becomes a female attribute. While Fuseli's public art attempted to cover up his sexual neuroses, it did not always succeed. In 1812, Benjamin Robert Haydon, an idealistic young artist who had fallen under Fuseli's influence, made the following entry in his diary: 'Think of Fuseli's savage ferocity, his whorish abandoned women, the daughters of the bawds of Hell, engendered by lecherous, dusky demons . . . I abhor Fuseli's mind, his subjects, and his manner; let me root his Pictures from my fancy forever, and banish them from my Soul.'

Τοιαδ ΕΠ ΕΧΘΡΧΙ Τουδ ΕΗΧδ ελθοι Κυπεις.

5

HENRY FUSELI (1741–1825)

Two Lesbians (1810–20)

Pen
$6\frac{7}{8} \times 4\frac{7}{8}$ in. (17.4 × 12.5 cm.)
Private collection

This beautiful drawing demonstrates the less ferocious side of Fuseli's erotic fantasy. While he might turn to Michelangelo and the Italian mannerists for the sense of strain and violence in their art (Plate 4), he could also turn to them for balletic anatomical grace. These long-necked ladies can be traced back to Parmigianino's sinuous, impossibly elongated types of female beauty. But where the Italian mannerists would twist and distort the human figure in order to prove their artistic still, Fuseli's anatomical inventiveness is a version of sexual play. His awkwardly positioned lesbian couple are absorbed less by physical contact (mouth to nipple, hand to vagina) than by their own image in the dressing-table mirror. They are narcissistic voyeurs, subordinating genital pleasure to the visual joys of an erotic *tableau vivant*. Fuseli had always been fascinated by the artistic and erotic possibilities of anatomical permutation. In Rome in the 1770s he had developed a curious drawing exercise, in which a male figure had to be drawn around five arbitrarily placed points, corresponding to head, hands and feet. This system was the ultimate extension of Fuseli's obsession with *maniera*, the virtuoso display of compositional ingenuity, but it also related to his sado-masochistic tendencies—the figure was placed in bondage, literally pinned down by the five points as surely as his man by three women (see Plate 4). Fuseli's lesbians, by contrast, are the mistresses of their own sexual contortions, deriving sexual fulfilment from the aesthetic arrangement of their bodies. Looking in a mirror, they are also mirror images of each other; the two girls share the same profile and coiffure, could almost be two versions of the same figure. In this light, the image becomes a fantasy of masturbation, a single girl absorbed in the sensuality of her reflection. Woman is the ruler of Fuseli's erotic universe, and as this image implies, she doesn't even need men to get her pleasure.

6

THOMAS ROWLANDSON
(1756–1827)

A Statuary's Yard (not dated)

Watercolour and pen and ink
6 × 9¼ in. (15 × 23.7 cm.)
Ashmolean Museum, Oxford

Fuseli is erotic art's tragedian, for whom sexuality is a compulsive, fatal flaw. Rowlandson, by contrast, offers a comic vision of *eros*—sex as liberator, freeing man from art into nature and a laughing recognition of his bodily desires. Rowlandson's roots lie in the naturalistic and comic traditions of art—the 'low-life' realism of Dutch painting; the witty eroticism of French Rococo (particularly Fragonard); Hogarth and the British tradition of graphic satire.

Rowlandson's *Statuary's Yard* is a playfully erotic reworking of an engraving produced by Hogarth to illustrate his aesthetic treatise *The Analysis of Beauty*. Hogarth's print was a sardonic comment on modern mannerisms, contrasted with the beautiful 'nature' of classical statuary—a posturing dancing master, for example, attempting to 'correct' the easy pose of a carved Antinous. Rowlandson extends the same contrast to satirize modern sexuality (or the lack of it). His statues are charged with sexual energy, whereas his human protagonists—with the exception of the coquettish girl on the old connoisseur's arm—are dessicated voyeurs. In the centre, the yard's proprietor points out an enticing Cupid and Psyche to two prospective clients. Statues make love, but connoisseurs prefer to watch—classical art becomes the eighteenth century's version of a sex peepshow. All around them, various forms of sexual dialogue develop. To their left, a pair of nudes are involved in amorous pursuit; to their right, a Venusian lady and her Adonis-like counterpart flirt from their respective plinths; further right, a nymph and satyr are locked in giggling embrace. Rowlandson reads antique art as an inventory of aphrodisiac delights. His statues are not frozen, but mobile erotic presences, possessed by the same fertile energies as the foliage in the background, where trees mimic the embraces of art.

7
GEORG EMANUEL OPITZ
(1775–1841)

The Tightrope (c. 1820)

Watercolour and pen and ink
9 × 7 in. (22.9 × 17.8 cm.)
Private collection

Opitz was a daughtsman and designer of engravings in the early part of the nineteenth century. He specialized in topographical and anecdoctal scenes, and settled in Leipzig in 1820. At around the same time he produced a series of erotic fantasies for private patrons, wittily pornographic compositions intended to arouse and amuse.

It seems very likely that Opitz knew Rowlandson's work (widely disseminated in engravings), and this watercolour, with its playful commentary on the joys of audience participation, continues many of Rowlandson's own erotic preoccupations. The theme of looking, of voyeurism as a surrogate sexual activity, is taken to the extreme by Opitz, whose audience mimics the activities of his athletic performers. Rowlandson had himself drawn an erotic tightrope scene; such images seem to have remained popular because they allow for maximum genital exposure. The sexual explicitness of the scene is defused by its comic absurdity. Opitz's drawing seeks to arouse (albeit jokily), and takes arousal for its subject. In the background, a group of musicians have erotically adapted their instruments: a drummer plays on a girl's back as they copulate, while to their right a man blows his trumpet through another girl's legs. (This is another theme popular with Rowlandson, who produced similar scenes of musicians 'tuning their instruments'.) In the foreground, an old gentleman is rejuvenated by his voyeurism. Opitz's watercolour is typical of the lighthearted erotic images that remained popular throughout the nineteenth and into the twentieth century.

8

THEODORE GERICAULT
(1791–1824)

Centaur Abducting a Woman
(1816–17)

Pen, wash and gouache
$6\frac{7}{8} \times 4\frac{7}{8}$ in. (17.5 × 12.5 cm.)
Louvre, Paris

In 1816, Theodore Gericault was already involved in the quasi-incestuous relationship with his maternal aunt that would plague him with guilt for the rest of his life. He left his native Paris, and escaped for a year of study in Italy. While he was in Rome, he produced a series of mythological erotic drawings, of which this is a fine example. Gericault is famous as French Romanticism's gloomy realist. While he kept to the forms of tradition, producing monumental history paintings, he subverted its values; there is nothing ideal or noble about Gericault's vision of man or the world, ruled by violence, misery and death.

On the surface, this sketch seems to signal a rare lightening of the artist's usual dark pessimism. Gericault, perhaps, is indulging in a nostalgic Rococo exercise, reviving the playful *eros* of Fragonard or Clodion. The amorous satyr or centaur with voluptuous maiden was a favourite motif in the Rococo period, when artists and sculptors used the contrast between hairy man-beast and beautiful girl to emphasize the smooth fleshy charms of their maidens. But Gericault phrases his erotic melée as struggle, where in Rococo art it would have been playful pursuit. His centaurs (one lies vanquished on the ground) are bestially impersonal. This is male sexuality as muscled domination, biological compulsion. Gericault uses touches of gouache to highlight their exaggerated musculature. His woman is expressionless, by contrast with the standard female erotic victim in Rococo art, who resists in her actions but complies in her coy gaze. Gericault's woman is locked in real combat. His drawing reminds us that in the Renaissance centaurs stood for man's lower, bestial nature; elsewhere in Gericault's work, the horse figures as a symbol of barely restrained sexuality or violence. Sex and guilt always seem linked in Gericault's universe—not until Picasso will we encounter such an intense, personal erotic vision drawn from the mythology of the past.

9

JEAN-FRANCOIS MILLET
(1814–1875)

The Lovers (1848–50)

Black crayon, stump, on yellowish paper
$12\frac{3}{4} \times 8\frac{5}{8}$ in. (32.4 × 22 cm.)
Art Institute of Chicago

Millet is best known for his radical and unsentimental images of agrarian poverty and hardship. Born into a family of prosperous peasants on the coast of Normandy, he drew on his own experience of rural activities like tilling or harvest-gathering as he evolved his uncompromising vision of man's relation to nature. Painted with a subdued palette, Millet's work is all earthy tones and textures; his figures, like the famous *Gleaners*, are bent to the ground in quest of sustenance. His paintings of rural poverty outraged right-wing critics when shown at the Paris *salons*, because they punctured the convenient establishment myth of a contented rustic population working in an arcadian landscape.

This tenderly erotic drawing, which probably dates from the years 1848–50, represents the obverse of Millet's harsh naturalism. Millet's workers are literally chained to their landscape by the need to survive, but his lovers inhabit a benevolent, protective nature. Shielded by the tree that arches over them, they embrace as innocently as entwined branches. Millet conceives their union as a process of organic growth—no urgent race to the satisfactions of climax, but a mute, stilled exploration. The man's right hand is buried in the shadow between the woman's legs, while the fingers of his left hand creep over her breast like tendrils. Millet's figures are generalized, anonymously idealized lovers, and, as if in recognition of the image's pastoral ideality, the artist has framed the drawing like an antique relief. On the one hand, Millet's figures are organic sexual presences; on the other, they are rendered as sculpture, an impossible ideal.

HONORE DAUMIER (1808–1879)

In the Kitchen (1863)

Pen and watercolour
$7\frac{1}{2} \times 9\frac{3}{4}$ in. (19 × 24.8 cm.)
Gichner Foundation for Cultural Studies

If Millet's *eros* springs from the twin conventions of classical statuary and pastoral, Daumier's is city-bred—harsh, lurid and unsentimental. *In the Kitchen* is something of an enigma in Daumier's *oeuvre*. Daumier produced very little erotic work, but this free pen and watercolour drawing, dated April 1863 and dedicated mysteriously to 'my good friend Louise' is a rare exception. Daumier was a witty and caustic commentator on his society's manners and *mores*, and a brilliant draughtsman. Apart from his numerous political cartoons, he produced many series of ironic lithographs in which he parodied the legal profession, the 'Bons Bourgeois' and the bluestockings of Parisian society (among many others). Baudelaire recognized his stature, and ranked him as a draughtsman with Delacroix and Ingres—'He draws as the great masters draw . . . He has a wonderful, almost divine memory, which for him takes the place of the model. All his figures stand firm on their feet, and their movement is always true'.

If *In the Kitchen* is intended as a satire, it is hard to pin down its object of attack—perhaps, as the dedication suggests, it is a private joke. Daumier observes his protagonists with a cartoonist's distance—his woman is a caricature of bovine receptivity, while his man fumbles urgently with his penis. Daumier's scrambled virtuosity of line is the index of these characters' absurd heatedness. He appears to have been uncertain over the drawing's composition, and ghostly traces of earlier poses survive (especially in the area around the man's left leg). Daumier's mastery of detail—the hanging pans and other clutter, the powerfully handled chimney recess—reminds us that this is a real kitchen, while the supine, plucked bird on the sideboard suggests a muted moral comment on the lovers' urgent, beast-like coupling. This low-life sexual encounter is the product of Daumier's urban vision; his lovers are a far cry from Millet's idealized inhabitants of pastoral.

11
JEAN-AUGUSTE-
DOMINIQUE INGRES
(1780–1867)

Bathing Scene (1864)

Engraving, pencil and watercolour
6½ × 5 in. (16.7 × 12.6 cm.)
Fogg Art Museum, Cambridge, Mass.

Ingres was eighty-four when he produced this watercolour, an enigmatic melange of oriental exoticism and linear austerity. It is an appeal to the senses: to sight, and to touch, in the sensuous figure of the central nude, who offers her curves to the spectator unaware; to hearing, in the music of the tambourine player and the gentle trickle of water into the bath; to taste and smell in the languorous coffee drinking to the bather's left. Yet while Ingres offers all this to the viewer, he holds him back from any sense of true participation. We are cast as outsiders by a series of pictorial strategies. The most obvious of Ingres' blocking devices is the arrangement of the composition: the broad expanse of the foreground nude's back marks the outermost point of a hermetic circle, within which the object of each nude's gaze is a mirror image, another nude. Ingres makes no appeal to a potentially salacious audience; his bathers are frozen in self-regarding stasis, stilled forever in an image that anticipates the pointillist eternities of Seurat. Ingres reinforces the coolness of this private universe by reminding us that this is *art*—the central bather is a direct copy of his *Valpincon Baigneuse*, painted some forty-six years earlier; the dancer to her right is recognizable as Angelica from Ingres' earlier mythological painting *Roger and Angelica*; the reclining nude to the left is a remodelled version of his *Odalisque with Slave*. Ingres has even created this image over an engraving, which he had already supervised, of the subject (by Reveil, who engraved most of Ingres' most famous works during the last decade of the artist's life). Ingres' watercolour, therefore, is not simply an image made up of prior representations in his *oeuvre*, it is even inscribed on the surface of a prior representation. Ingres distances eroticism, classically purifies it, by a double closure of the image—the spectator is kept back by the composition (and the refrigerated colour scheme), and further reminded that these are figures from the Ingres canon.

12

EDGAR DEGAS (1834–1917)

Admiration (c. 1880)

Monotype, black ink on pale white paper
with two light touches of colour
$8\frac{1}{2} \times 6\frac{3}{8}$ in.(21.5 × 16.1 cm.)
Bibliothèque d'Art et d'Archaeologie
de France, Paris

Degas was first introduced to Ingres in 1855, and he frequently recalled the older master's words of advice: 'Draw lines, lots of lines, either from memory or nature. Degas mastered the art of draughtmanship, but he put it to the service of an art very different to Ingres' rigorously refined classicism. By the early 1880s, when he produced this monotype, Degas had abandoned the style and ambitions of his early Ingres-inspired portraits and history paintings, and had evolved an art that aimed to reflect modern life. 'It is odd to think', he remarked in old age, 'that in another era I would have painted Susannah and the Elders.' *Admiration* is one of a number of pastelled monotypes by Degas in which he depicted the interiors of contemporary Parisian brothels. The monotype medium could not be executed on the spot, so Degas was certainly working from memory (as Ingres had suggested) as well as from nature. He enjoyed the textural effects made possible by monotype, the impression it gives of an image snatched in haste. Space is flattened in *Admiration* (the wash stand appears to tip forward from the picture plane), turning the background into a patterned screen of descriptive marks that throw the figures into relief. One can detect the influence of Japanese prints on Degas here, and indeed the theme of carefully posed bathing women and prostitutes is part of the Japanese Ukiyo-e tradition. The nature of the image's eroticism remains ambiguous—how much of himself does Degas put into his crouching, bearded figure? On the evidence of the gently, sensuously modelled female nude, and his generally subdued rendering of the whole scene, Degas implies a distance between the artist and his leering ogler. Degas' voyeurism seems a gentle, almost aesthetic affair. Picasso offered his own view of Degas in a late series of etchings on the theme of famous artists and their models: Raphael paints the Fornarina as he has sex with her, but a smartly dressed, rather formal Degas watches from one side as naked women display themselves extravagantly. Even in this uncharacteristically overt brothel scene, Degas himself seems detached, an artist keeping his distance.

13
AUBREY BEARDSLEY
(1872–1898)

Cinesias Entreating Myrrhina
to Coition (1896)

Pen and ink
$10\frac{1}{4} \times 7$ in. (26 × 18 cm.)
Victoria and Albert Museum, London

Aubrey Beardsley illustrated Aristophanes' lewd comedy *Lysistrata* in 1896 for a limited edition of the play printed by the publisher Leonard Smithers. At the time of the commission Beardsley seems to have regarded it as a liberating opportunity—he wrote jokily to Smithers in a letter accompanying one of the drawings, 'The rampant Athenians', that 'if there are no cunts in the picture Aristophanes is to blame and not your humble servant'.

The scene illustrated here shows one of those rampant Athenians, Cinesias, begging his wife Myrrhina for sexual favours. She is resisting him, about to rejoin the Athenian wives in Aristophanes' play who have joined Lysistrata's sex strike (in order to force their husbands to abandon the war against Sparta). Aristophanes' comedy is an appropriate subject for Beardsley to illustrate, since its subject is the endless deferral of the sexual act. Critics who have frowned on drawings like this one for their crude or pornographic intent miss the point—the *Lysistrata* drawings merely underline Beardsley's inability to dramatize the sexual act, are poignant comments on his own tubercular impotence. Sex in Beardsley is always displaced, transmuted to fetish—this image, despite Cinesias' swollen phallus, is just such an exercise in fetishism. Cinesias contacts not Myrrhina's body but her clothes: his penis is caressed by the dangling tassels of her cloak, while his extended arm and grasping hand (which, with their elaborate ruff, echo the shape of his phallus) touch fabric, not flesh. The only part of Myrrhina that actually reaches out towards Cinesias is her diaphanous scarf, fluttering backwards to touch his erectile feathered headress, as if her clothes alone countenance a union which she rejects. Even Cinesias' extravagant member does less to reinforce a sense of sexual reality than fantasy; it is, literally, a dream of a penis. The artists of the aesthetic movement preferred art to nature—Beardsley's image extends that preference to sex, finding eroticism less palatable in the bodies of its participants than in the more decorous intercourse of their elaborate, excitingly drawn accoutrements.

14
AUGUSTE RODIN (1840–1917)

Two Women (c. 1900–10)

Pencil, watercolour, gouache on
cream paper
12⅝ × 9½ in. (32 × 24 cm.)
Musée Rodin, Paris

In 1900 Rodin exhibited all his major sculptures at the International Exposition in Paris, establishing his status as the greatest sculptor of his time. In the years that followed, until his death in 1917, he shifted his interest to the expressive possibilities of drawing. In the last twenty years of his life, he produced thousands of sketches, of which almost all explore erotic themes. Rodin filled his studio with female models, whom he encouraged to assume a variety of acrobatic or erotic poses. Both choreographer and draughtsman, Rodin sketched them as they moved, without looking down at his paper. He described his ambitions at some length: 'I have, as it were, to *incorporate* the lines of the human body, and they must become part of myself, deeply seated in my instincts . . . Not a thought about the technical problem of representing it on paper could be allowed to arrest the flow of my feelings about it, from my eye to my hand. The moment I drop my eyes the flow stops.'

Rodin would go through his original, spontaneous sketches, and make a tracing of the essential lines—the drawing reproduced here, of two women in each other's arms, is almost certainly such a tracing. Unlike Klimt (whom he influenced) Rodin defines form in single lines—no caressing, dwelling linear repetitions here, but a hectic, gestural incorporation of the models' motions into his own body. Where Klimt establishes a sense of distance, his own male presence as viewer (and enjoyer) of female form (Fig. 8 and Plate 16), Rodin literally tries to become the bodies he is drawing—the scribbled lines that halo the two heads of his figures remind us of Rodin's own intense bodily activity. The eroticism of this image inheres in a curious sense of sexual energy transferred from models to artist. Rodin seeks a strange sexual rejuvenation through art in its most basic form, the gesture.

Hommage
à ma grande amie
Judith Cladel
Aug. Rodin

7195

15

EDVARD MUNCH (1863–1944)

Man and Woman (1912–15)

Watercolour and charcoal
$23\frac{5}{8} \times 31\frac{3}{8}$ in. (59.9 × 79.6 cm.)
Munch Museum, Oslo

Munch's gloomily Nordic vision of the human condition was dominated by sexual anxiety. Munch's women fall into the categories designated by the nervous misogynists of Symbolist and Decadent art—betrayers of men (Salome, Eve) or vulnerable adolescents. In Munch's world sexuality is a force for evil, bound up with the depressing material and biological determinism of the new science. Woman is the instrument of an inevitable biological curse, as she chains man to his bodily desires.

Although Munch was softening this pessimistic vision at the time when he created this drawing, his impassive and aloof woman is still very much in the mould of *femme fatale*. Her long black hair links her with Munch's threatening *Madonna* lithograph of 1896, while the drawing's nervously striated and scribbled lines are signals of the artist's unease. Hair in Munch is a powerful symbol of woman's sexual potency, the rope by which she binds her victims, or the web into which she absorbs them. Sexual encounter is an act of vampirism—the surrender of male identity in lust, the absorption of man by woman (Munch's male figure is significantly faceless, his profile lost in a blur of reddish watercolour). Munch's fidgety line suggests psychic anxiety, a troubled superfluity of marks that play no part in description. This is not a tender image, and it recalls Munch's statement that 'I have never loved. I have experienced the passion that can move mountains and transform people—the passion that tears at the heart and drinks one's blood. But there has never been anyone to whom I could say—Woman, it is you I love'.

16

GUSTAV KLIMT (1862–1918)

Reclining Woman (1912–18)

Coloured pencil
14⅝ × 22 in. (37.1 × 56 cm.)
Albertina, Vienna

Gustav Klimt's finest erotic drawings date from the last decade of his life. The artist in his studio surrounded himself with nude models, whom he arranged and sketched in a bewildering array of poses. Klimt's preoccupation with human sexuality had already led him into controversy in his public career. Between 1900 and 1903 he had offended critics and the general public alike, when he exhibited the large oil paintings commissioned by Vienna University to decorate its great hall. Although these were allegorical works on general themes, Klimt framed his vision of man in threatening, pessimistically sexual terms—*Medicine*, in particular, aroused bourgeois disgust, with its uncompromising portrayal of the human life cycle as a struggling orgy of sexual activity. Klimt withdrew the paintings but refused to change his subject matter.

As this drawing demonstrates, Klimt's eroticism underwent a profound shift in his later years. Klimt moved from the aggressive stance of his earlier allegorical work to a utopian, panerotic vision, in which woman becomes both object of desire and Edenic landscape. He was certainly influenced by Rodin's late drawings. Like Rodin, Klimt was fascinated by the infinite multiplicity of the body's poses—this is not an academic nude. But where Rodin's gestural technique literally mirrors the actions of his models, Klimt's line dwells on and restates form, caressing rather than galvanizing (note the sensual linear repetitions of the girl's shins, feet and ankles). Correspondingly, where Rodin's models are acrobatic, Klimt's are languorous—the girl here is lethargic, her masturbation a gentle act of self-exploration that matches the caresses of Klimt's graphic technique.

17

EGON SCHIELE (1890–1918)

Lovers (1911)

Pencil, gouache
19 × 12 in. (48.3 × 30.5 cm.)
Fischer Fine Art, London

Egon Schiele would have succeeded Klimt as Vienna's leading *avant-garde* painter, had he not died in 1918 at the age of twenty eight, victim of the same influenza epidemic that killed the older master. In 1907 Schiele met Klimt for the first time and presented him with a portfolio of drawings, asking 'Do I have talent?' 'Yes! Much too much!' came the reply, and the artists became friends. Like Klimt, Schiele was fascinated by erotic subjects; but where Klimt's eroticism is a tender celebration of beauty, literally caressing his models with the flowing, rounded lines of his drawing, Schiele seems anxious and neurotic.

The watercolour reproduced here is one of a series of images of young girls produced by the artist in 1911 in Neulengbach, a small Austrian town where he scandalized the inhabitants by living with his mistress-cum-model Wally Neuzill. In 1912, drawings like this one were produced as evidence when Schiele was put on trial for alleged seduction of a minor. While awaiting trial, he kept a prison diary, in which he recorded his sexual anxieties: 'I believe that man must suffer from sexual torture as long as he is capable of sexual feelings'. Schiele seems fascinated by the vulnerability of pubescent sexuality; dwelling on bony protuberances, the emaciated curves of skinny thighs and buttocks, his line exaggerates the frailty of these young girls. While Schiele inherits from Klimt his fascination with quasi-abstract pattern (in the checks and frills of the girls' dresses), the drawing's atmosphere of erotic malaise, conveyed by pinched, mottled flesh, is all his own. Schiele was obsessed with young girls, but this image suggests that his obsession stemmed less from desire than from his perception of them as awkward, angular embodiments of his own troubled sexuality.

18

ERNST LUDWIG KIRCHNER
(1880–1938)

A Couple (1908)

Black and coloured chalks on paper
34⅞ × 27 in. (88.5 × 68.5 cm.)
Brücke-Museum, Berlin

In 1905 Ernst Ludwig Kirchner became one of the founder members of a radical group of artists in Dresden. Calling themselves 'Die Brücke' (the bridge) and drawing their inspiration from the Expressionists, they aimed to break away from the past and build a bridge to the art of the future. 'As youth, we carry the future', declared Kirchner in the group's manifesto, 'and we want to create for ourselves freedom of life and movement against the long-entrenched forces of seniority. Everyone who reveals his creative drives with authenticity and directness belongs with us.' The free expression of sexuality was *de rigueur*: numerous photographs survive of Kirchner's studio, peopled by nude men and women who pose or dance in front of the photographer as they would before the artist. Kirchner and his circle tried to evolve an art that would parallel the calculated spontaneity of their lives. From 1906 onwards he sketched incessantly, never working on a drawing for more than ten or fifteen minutes—he would later state that 'the sole aim of art is to express life by pure tones and simple forms'.

Drawing is the natural medium for Kirchner's aesthetic of erotic immediacy. This drawing, of two of the artist's (unidentified) friends, dates from 1908. The bright colours and expressive distortions of anatomy testify to Kirchner's fascination with Matisse and the Fauves at this time. Raoul Dufy, one of the first of the Fauves, once asked the rhetorical question 'How . . . can I render, not what I see, but what is, what exists for me, my reality?' In this image we find Kirchner engaged in the same quest, experimenting with the possibilities of a purely subjective art—the drawing preserves the energy of his response to these nudes in its flowing contours and near-abstract scribbles of colour (Kirchner also admired Gothic and African art for what he saw as emotionally expressive primitivism).

In the end, his insistence on an art of continual nervous response bred neuroses. After a series of mental breakdowns, Kirchner suffered the final indignity of being branded 'degenerate' by the Nazis in 1937. The following year, he killed himself.

19

AMEDEO MODIGLIANI

(1884–1920)

Caryatid (*c.* 1913–15)

Pastel and crayon with wash
20⅞ × 19 in. (53 × 48.2 cm.)
Musée de l'Art Moderne de la
Ville de Paris

Amedeo Modigliani probably executed this exquisite pastel, crayon and wash drawing between 1913 and 1915. Modigliani had little formal artistic training. He arrived in Paris in 1906, where the impact of advanced contemporary art catalyzed his rapid development into one of the major figures of the Parisian school. He was immediately influenced by the smooth surfaces and organic shapes of Brancusi's sculpture—until 1915, he regarded himself primarily as a sculptor. Like Brancusi and Picasso, who first experimented with tribal figures in his art between 1906 and 1908, Modigliani was fascinated by the forms of African sculpture. But where Picasso turns to African art in quest of savage vitality, Modigliani adapts the new visual language to express a cool, almost classical eroticism.

This drawing exaggerates the fertile curves of belly, thighs and arms, but Modigliani contains the sensuality of these elements within a line as pure as Ingres'. There is a trace, too, of Renaissance or Mannerist artifice in the nude's elegantly twisted *contrapposto*. Modigliani's grey-blue ground recalls the tonalities of Cezanne, the most classical of late Impressionists. The eroticism of this drawing is suspended between the voluptuousness of a rounded, exaggerated anatomy, and its expression as pure form, a rhythm of linear curves on a cool field of colour.

20

GEORGE GROSZ (1893–1959)

Strength and Beauty (1922)

Watercolour, pen and ink
21 × 17⅜ in. (53.3 × 44 cm.)
Wallraf-Richartz Museum, Cologne

George Grosz's Berlin is a twentieth-century version of Bosch's hell. Peopled by vampish whores, fat, cigar-smoking capitalists, war cripples, sex murderers and thuggish soldiers, this is a world where corruption is the only rule. Grosz saw himself as a moral reformer, a satirist who sought to purge the world of evil by laying bare its degeneracy. 'My art', he stated in his autobiography, 'was to be a gun and a sword; my drawing pens I declared to be empty straws as long as they did not take part in the fight for freedom.'

Grosz's man and woman are rendered in the cruel lines of satire. Their self-images have turned them into caricatures, as the drawing's title ironically points out. The bullet-headed industrialist has adopted an arrogantly rakish pose, but his posturing makes him an embodiment of brutishness not strength. Like most of Grosz's businessmen he has the features of a pig and the cranial formation of the criminally subnormal. Grosz's whore sees herself as a provocative beauty, but her languor and dishevelment seem the products of alcoholism rather than sensuality (Grosz has carefully included incriminating bottles on her dressing table to explain her rolling eyes and fixed grin). This couple are not so much sexual partners as links in a chain of parasitism—the industrialist feeds off the workers, while the whore feeds off him. By choosing to place his drawing in post-coital time Grosz underlines the soulless and mercenary nature of their sexual transaction.

21

EDWARD BURRA (1905–1976)

The Tea Shop (1929)

Pencil and gouache
26 × 18¾ in. (66 × 47.6 cm.)
Private collection

George Melly touchingly described Burra a few years before his death, voicing camp welcomes to his friends in 'a selfmade Cockney drawl like an elderly but game Edwardian tart propositioning from the shadows'. While Burra kept up a brave show of camp wit in his late years, his youth was an irreverent and excited period of exploration. Burra spent much of the 1920s in the Mediterranean South, fascinated by the seamy side of life in Marseilles, Toulon or Barcelona. Eroticism filtered through into his art—less, one feels, through compulsion than through a naive and eager desire to *épater les bourgeois*.

The Tea Shop is an exuberant conflation of middle-class haven and Burra's beloved girlie revue. *Eros* is a jokey presence in the picture, these ludicrously made-up and decked-out waitresses who mock their clientele by drenching them with tea and milk. Burra loved decadence: his tea shop is a crazy, brothel-like place, where a tree can sprout lightbulbs, women smoke (bad taste in the Twenties) and a flowerpot stand grows arms and legs. Burra was influenced at this time by German *Neue Sachlichkeit* painting, the harsh satires of George Grosz or Otto Dix—the male physiognomies in this picture look distinctly Germanic. But Burra's image entirely lacks the virulence of the German artists. His grotesque sexpots are fondly observed. This is a manically erotic image, the expression of youthful high spirits.

22
ROJAN (active 1930–1950)

Scene from Idylle Printanière
(*c.* 1935)

Lithograph and crayon
6¾ × 6⅛ in. (17 × 15.5 cm)
Private collection

Rojan was one of several French illustrators who supplied the erotic marketplace in Paris between the wars. Little is known about him—his real name was possibly Rojankowski; he was possibly Polish; and he is thought to have left France for America in about 1955. Rojan's anonymity extends to his artwork—this is not the kind of erotic image that tells us about its creator. Nor is it intended to—this is a commercial exercise, the kind of pornographic work that has now been superseded by the colour photograph, the blue movie or video.

Rojan's lovers in their taxicab, too absorbed by desire to notice the busy traffic or the gesturing gendarme outside, are framed like a photographic still. This is not actually a drawing, but a lithograph, hand-coloured by the artist in crayon. It is one of a series of thirty, which recount the rudimentary narrative of a couple's erotic *rendezvous*, from pick-up, through to taxi-ride, to the final consummation of their passion in a hotel. Rojan's format is designed for pornographic consumption—some of his images act as narrative fillers, while others (like this one) are designed for lingering delectation. Rojan is an illustrator, and his graphic technique is as standard as his characters, sexual surrogates for the consumer. The modern viewer is likely to find this image quaint or amusing—perhaps because we are unused to seeing mainstream Thirties illustrative style put to erotic use, as if the stylish rendering of contemporary fashion (the man's Homburg, the girl's fox-fur and dainty shoes and stockings) were somehow out of place in so overtly an erotic scene. Through its failure (in modern eyes) as pornography, Rojan's image acquires a kind of dated, titillating charm.

23
PABLO PICASSO (1881–1973)

Minotaur and Nude (1933)

India ink on blue paper
18½ × 24⅜ in. (47 × 62 cm.)
Art Institute of Chicago

Picasso is the giant of twentieth-century art. He has attained near-mythical status as the eternally potent artist and procreator, and as the inventor of a thousand styles. But against this twin myth, Picasso as symbol of virility, Picasso as propagator of endless new 'styles', it is important to remember how compulsively confessional his art was, and how frequently it confessed a deeply neurotic attitude to sex.

Picasso completed this drawing in the summer of 1933, when his collapsing marriage was in its worst period of crisis. Picasso's art underwent a metamorphosis in the 1930s. In the 1920s, shortly after his marriage to Olga Koklova, Picasso produced a series of monumental and serene classicizing works in which he celebrated woman as a statuesque maternal archetype; in the 1930s his neuroses surfaced in a series of images that define sex as warfare. The minotaur becomes a favourite symbol of male sexuality. Here it appears as masculine avenger, but also as the slave of its own bestial appetites. The forms, in their dense and sculptural heaviness, recall the figure types of Picasso's 'classical' period, but they have been galvanized by an extraordinary, almost animal energy. Picasso's drawing is an orgy of harsh linear scribbling, which suggests not only the violence of this rape but also the violent artistic activity that went into the image.

The minotaur is an ancient symbol of untamed sexual and murderous instincts. Athenian youths and maidens were sacrificed to the beast by King Minos, but Theseus and Ariadne eventually defeated it and its labyrinth, a victory for classical valour and reason. When Picasso chooses the minotaur as his alter-ego he turns his back on classicism and reaches towards irrationality, embracing a type of primitive bestialism.

24

HANS BELLMER (1902–1975)

A Woman from the Back (1943)

Coloured pencils
11½ × 14½ in. (29.5 × 36.5 cm.)
Private collection

Hans Bellmer began his artistic career in 1933 when he constructed the first of his 'Dolls'—'an artificial girl with anatomical possibilities which are capable of re-creating the heights of passion even to inventing new desires', as he described her. Bellmer made his doll from detritus—broom handle, metal nuts and bolts—and modelled her torso and head in plaster of Paris that resembled rotting flesh. When the Surrealists saw photographs of his work they heralded the arrival of a new genius and welcomed him into their group.

Bellmer uses the irrational and metamorphic devices of surrealist art to express his strange and intense sexual imagination. In his theoretical writings he proposed the existence of a 'purely subjective, imaginary' anatomy of the human body, the erotic anatomy we find in this disquieting drawing of 1943. Bellmer reinvents the body as a fluid product of desire. It becomes the site of infinite sexual displacements: his woman's hair coils pubically over a neck that snakes into a phallus; her shoulders melt backwards to form nippled mounds of flesh; she sprouts several pairs of rubbery, parted legs, while her fingers probe an orifice, at once anus and vagina. Flesh takes on a life of its own, rolling, bending and dripping to create suggestive hollows or protuberances. Bellmer's graphic techniques—superimposition, metamorphosis—make the human body a vehicle for the artist's endless inventory of erotic imaginings. The inexhaustibility of Bellmer's fantasy is not the sign of vitality but of a restless spirit's failure to find satisfaction. In the end, Bellmer is a gloomy libertine, trapped in his own sexual labyrinth.

25
ARSHILE GORKY (1904–1948)
The Garden of Sochi (1941)

Gouache on paper
$13\frac{3}{4} \times 17\frac{3}{4}$ in. (34.9 × 45.1 cm.)
Private collection

Gorky's paintings of the Garden of Sochi are among his most personal works. They evoke childhood memories of his father's garden in Gorky's native Armenia—'the garden of wish-fulfilment', as he described it in a poem written to explain their sensuous imagery. This is a rare gouache in the series (most were painted in oils). In 1941 Gorky was on the brink of developing an artistic language to express his personal perception of nature, but he had not yet thrown off the influence of other artists—*The Garden of Sochi* shows the strong influence of the Catalan painter Joan Miro's language of abstract forms. Gorky adopts Miro's biomorphic forms, transmuting their overt sexual references into a fluid and ambiguous eroticism.

Gorky's nature is all buttocky clefts and probing, phallic tendrils, the world as fecundating plasma. The heavy form at the picture's centre is a metamorphic image of abstract sexuality, at once breast, buttocks, vagina, fruit and testes. Gorky wrote a poem related to the Garden of Sochi series in which he juxtaposed 'the shape of apricots, those flirts of the sun', and 'the soft and dependant breasts' of women. In 1942 he wrote a letter to his sister in which he declared, 'in trying to probe beyond the ordinary and the human, I create an inner infinity'. Gorky's dream-like forms suggest a correspondence between external nature and an equivalent landscape of human sexual parts, a strange and powerfully erotic vision. Elaine de Kooning's description of Gorky's later work applies, too, to this picture—'forms change, as you look, into a cruel and opulent sexual imagery'.

26
WILLEM DE KOONING
(1904–)

Two Women (1952)

Pastel
$8\frac{1}{2} \times 24\frac{5}{8}$ in. (47 × 62.5 cm.)
Art Institute of Chicago

De Kooning's *Two Women* is one of many drawings and pastels he produced in the two and a half years of trial and error that led to his great painting *Woman 1*. De Kooning began by attempting to create his version of the all-American girl—a cross between Marilyn Monroe, the girl in the old Camel cigarette adverts, and Doris Day. He himself was surprised by the threatening, totemic figures he created—looking back on these works in 1960, De Kooning commented 'I look at them now and they seem vociferous and ferocious. I think it had to do with the idea of the idol, the oracle, and above all the hilariousness of it.'

De Kooning's hectic, improvisatory manipulations of pastel reinforce his image's appearance as a mass of almost incidental marks, a continuous field of gestural activity. Yet the disturbing power of these exaggerated female anatomies comes from their emergence, as crudely modelled representational forms, out of a blurred and scratchy abstract ground. More precisely, this is a form of archaeological eroticism; as if De Kooning has dug these bikini-girls-cum-primitive-harpies out of some primal landscape. If these figures are awkwardly hilarious, as the artist suggests, they are also the creations of anxiety. De Kooning's lines seem to have been taken over by an obsessive misogynist fear, locating in Woman a scary, faceless creature all procreative parts—jutting hips, belly, buttocks and those scalloped, massy breasts. Significantly, de Kooning began his move away from the *Woman* series with a painting titled *Woman as Landscape*. As Harry Gaugh has commented, 'De Kooning painted himself away from Woman by ploughing her under as landscape'; reversing the archaeological processes of his art, he freed himself from these disturbing visions.

27

TOM WESSELMANN (1931–   )

Study for Great American Nude
(1966)

Pencil and liquitex
9 × 13½ in. (23 × 34.5 cm.)
Private collection

Like De Kooning, Tom Wesselmann the American Pop artist draws his inspiration from the pin-up. But where De Kooning turns her into a malevolent fiend, Wesselmann tames her, makes her a source of endless male gratification. The pencil and liquitex drawing reproduced here is a study for one of Wesselmann's numerous monumental paintings of the female nude, *Great American Nude No. 91* of 1967. This image shows the influence of early twentieth-century masters, incorporating the extravagant colour and linear virtuosity of Matisse within a strictly controlled compositional framework that derives ultimately from Mondrian. Wesselmann aimed at immediacy and vitality, while eschewing the gestural painterly exuberance of Abstract Expressionists like De Kooning. In his own words 'Colours became flatter, cleaner, brighter; edges became harder, clearer . . . I felt the need to lock up my paintings so tightly that nothing could move. This way, by becoming static and somewhat anonymous, they also became more charged with energy.'

The woman's anonymity is the key to this drawing. Pop artists were fascinated by the idea of technology, which in the Sixties seemed to offer a utopian Disneyland of consumer durables. Wesselmann turns woman into a user-friendly sex object. He takes the pin-up, the ideal girlfriend, and converts her coy promise of sexual gratification into a reality—an expressionless, splayed availability of vagina and mouth. He reverses the function of the pin-up's bikini, designed to cover up those parts of her body we can only dream about (pornography was still virtually illegal in America in 1966): the lines produced by his nude's suntan isolate her breasts and genitals and thus emphasize her purely sexual role. The colours underline her status as all-American sex toy—red white and blue of the American flag with gold (the artist explains) referring to the fringe on most flags. Later in his career Wesselmann would dream of art collages that would incorporate real nude women hired by the gallery and alternating in shifts, the ultimate extension of the woman as sex object we find in this drawing.

28

ALLEN JONES (1937–)

Desire Me (1968)

Pencil and ballpen on cartridge paper,
with airbrushed photograph
38 × 15¾ in. (96.5 × 40 cm.)
Victoria and Albert Museum, London

In 1974, six years after he had created this image, Allen Jones conducted a mock-interview with his own work of art. Writing under the scurrilous pseudonym I. Seymour-Legge, Jones asked his drawing if she considered herself a real woman. 'I am a sign for one', he had her reply, 'call it Art if you like'. Jones has been criticized in the past as Pop Art's erotic salesman, a purveyor of sexist male fantasies, but to view his work in those terms is to miss its point. Jones has always been fascinated by the instant appeal of mass imagery—mail order catalogues are key sources for his work, especially those designed to sell fetish or 'glamour' footwear. *Desire Me*, like many of Jones' titles, is the name of a style of leather boot. Jones' drawing is more than an alluring pin-up; it is a cleverly ambiguous work of art that forces the viewer to acknowledge the artifice of an erotic prototype.

The lower half of *Desire Me* is an invitation to tactile response. It is actually a photograph of an earlier oil-painting by Jones, *Wet Seal*, touched up by airbrush to enhance the sleek realism of the girl's pneumatic left leg. Jones plays games with the erotic accessibility of his image; as our gaze travels upwards, his lady undergoes a metamorphosis from skintight glossiness to linear shorthand. The image reminds us of its own status as fantasy—deprived of her fetishistic armour, this girl turns into a phantom, a series of ghostly contours. If we want her whole body to live up to the glamorous perfection of her legs, we will have to complete her rubber coating in our imaginations. By inviting our participation in the image's fetish, and by using more than one visual convention (perspective, line) Jones examines the way sexual fantasy operates.

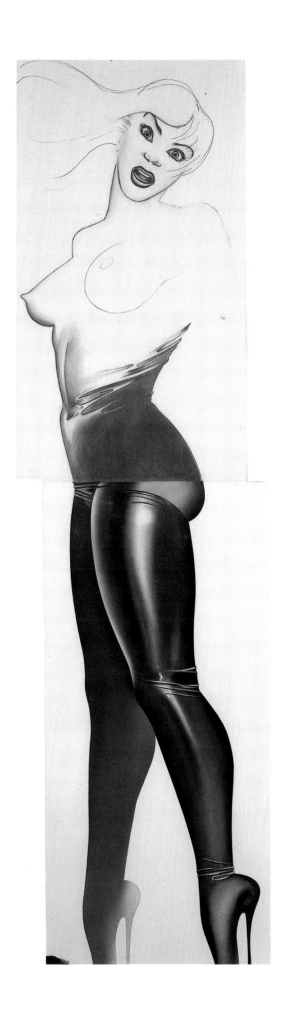

29

DAVID HOCKNEY (1937–)

Bob on 'The France' (1963)

Colour crayon and pencil on paper
$19\frac{1}{8} \times 20\frac{1}{8}$ in. (48.5 × 51 cm.)
Private collection

Like Allen Jones, his contemporary at the Royal College of Art, David Hockney is interested in popular erotic imagery. In an interview with Peter Webb, Hockney acknowledged his admiration of drawings in American gay magazines by artists like Tom of Finland and Spartacus—'beautiful muscular men in leather or in the nude'. But as this delicately homo-erotic pencil and crayon drawing shows, Hockney's art does not deal in sexual stereotypes. Where Allen Jones forces us to question the visual strategies of such stereotypes, Hockney is more interested in the gentle observation of a particular young man's body.

Hockney drew this image from life on board a ship returning to England in 1965. The man's face-down pose is a favourite with the artist (it predicts his 1967 painting *The Room, Tarzana*), giving prominence to the buttocks. Hockney's draughtsmanship is economical to the point of austerity— barely indicating bed and setting, he concentrates on the outline rather than the fleshly texture of the man's vulnerable, sleeping anatomy. This creates a sense of stillness, the moment of quiet in which the artist has chosen to make his sketch. The drawing's erotic charge derives from the tension between outline and inflamed colour, the blocks of pink shading which emphasize those areas of the man's body that arouse the artist's desire. This emphasis is underscored by the way in which Hockney loses interest in the man's right thigh as it moves away from his buttocks, not bothering to complete the rest of the leg. Hockney's eros is leisurely and untroubled. His drawing is at once a gesture of desire and restraint, sensual colour played off against fastidious draughtsmanship.

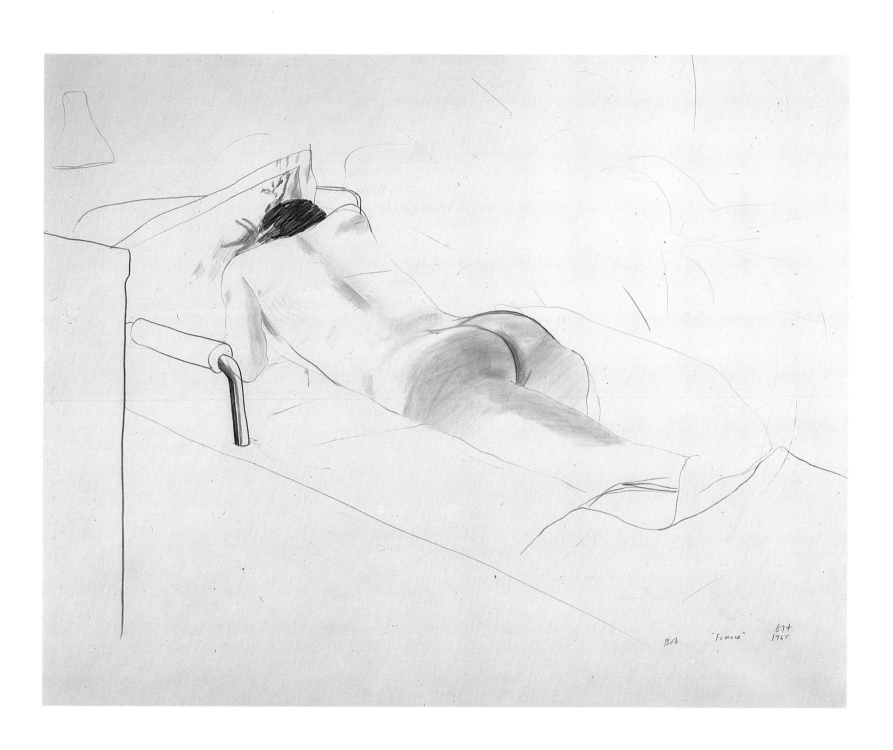

Bob   "France"   67+
1965

30

NANCY GROSSMAN (1940–)

Figure (1970)

Ink on paper
$45\frac{1}{2} \times 34\frac{1}{2}$ in. (115.6 × 87.6 cm.)
Princeton Art Museum, Princeton

Nancy Grossman is an American artist probably best known for her disturbing and fetishistic leather sculptures. These are usually male heads, presented on plinths like grisly relics of decapitation. They are bound, blinded and muzzled by extraordinary leather face masks, all straps, studs and zips. Like the British Pop artist Allen Jones, Grossman draws her inspiration from the imagery of the sexual underground. Her masks are over-the-top variants of articles sold by sex shops catering to the sado-masochistic market, and sometimes she actually uses commercially manufactured leather hoods in her work.

In large drawings like this one Grossman takes the surreal potential of bondage fetishism to fantastic extremes. The figure here is literally the slave of his desires: his hands are cuffed together, his arms cruelly pinioned behind his back by a leather strap that compresses his powerfully muscled shoulders, while his head has been engulfed by a savage mask, half gun, half beastly predator. Grossman's work has perhaps predictably been interpreted as vengeful feminism, sexual exploitation with the tables turned on men. But she insists on its compassion, and describes her creatures as victims of sexual taboo—'a taboo against living: to have a head and no feelings, to have a vagina and not fill it, to have a penis and not stick it in—that is not living.' In this light the poignancy of Grossman's image begins to emerge. Sexual obsession breeds incapacity, a loss of identity in fetish metaphorically underlined by the way in which the man's face has been literally devoured by the violent features of his mask. This loss of self constitutes the real (and intentional) obscenity of the image.

31

R B KITAJ (1932–)

This Knot of Life (1975)

Pastel on paper
$15\frac{1}{4} \times 22\frac{1}{2}$ in. (38.7 × 57.2 cm.)
Collection of the Artist

In the Seventies Kitaj abandoned the collage techniques of his earlier, Pop-influenced work and devoted himself to figurative art. *This Knot of Life*, like nearly all Kitaj's erotic pastels, dates from the mid-Seventies. His work is frequently literary and allusive; to understand this particular image the viewer needs to know something of Kitaj's personal mythology. Much of his work is obsessed with the decay of urban civilization; Kitaj is fond of references to Eliot's *Waste Land*, and to Walter Benjamin, the wandering Jew bringing his keen intellect to bear on the collapsing society that surrounds him.

Kitaj's voyeur in this pastel is perhaps a version of this central figure, the artist's alter-ego as Benjamin. Like Degas, Kitaj is fascinated by the twin themes of voyeurism and the brothel, but where Degas is a cool, detached observer, Kitaj introduces a moral element. In an interview in 1981 he talked about the brothel and 'its hellish sighs at the heart of decaying cities'. His monochrome ghost in the hallway, gazing at the copulating couple, acts as condemnatory presence—a philosophical observer of decadence. Kitaj's pastel technique is vastly (and self-confessedly) indebted to Degas. But the cinematic feel of the image (and the way in which the couple almost look like a projected slide) is reminiscent of Edward Hopper's visions of urban alienation. Many of Kitaj's overtly sexual *mises-en-scene* are culled directly from commercial pornography, and his couple are stock pornographic figures. This distances them still further from their shadowy spectator, and from the viewer, for whom he is a surrogate. They become stereotypes of crude sexuality, symptoms (in Kitaj's own mythology) of *eros* as a weakening and destructive force. The title refers to Cleopatra's instructions to the asp that will kill her (from Shakespeare): 'With thy sharp teeth this knot intrinsicate/Of life at once untie'. Kitaj's *Knot of Life* is the pair of grappling lovers; he implies that their sexuality is also a force for death, a metaphorical serpent.

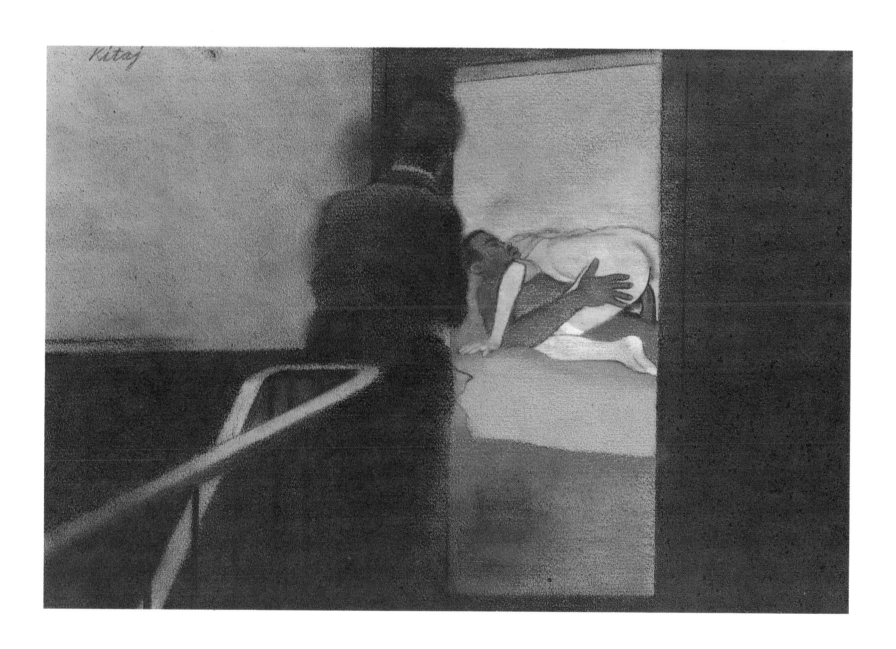

32

SANDRA FISHER (1947–   )

Dying Slave (1979)

Pastel on paper
18½ × 12⅞ in. (47 × 32.7 cm.)
Private collection, England

This book began with Boucher's drawing of a sleeping girl, an image designed to cater to male sexual fantasy. It is appropriate that it should end with Sandra Fisher's delicate pastel of a sleeping man—the tables turned. Fisher herself describes sleep as a state of erotic vulnerability—'because this man is asleep, fantasy is allowed free rein'. She is married to Kitaj, and first introduced him to pastel as a medium. But where Kitaj's erotic art is complicated by his slowly evolved, personal symbolism, Fisher's seems more direct—this image is composed with deliberate artfulness, certainly, but its eroticism derives from the sexually charged observation and rendering of a specific male body. The drawing's title, 'Dying Slave', reminds us of its inspiration in the art of Michelangelo: the model's pose copies Michelangelo's *Dying Slave* (in the Louvre), and Fisher has even wittily echoed the band of drapery across the chest of Michelangelo's sculpture in her own model's rucked-up T-shirt. But where Michelangelo uses that drapery to emphasize the dynamic energy of his sculpture, suggesting that his figure's heroic anatomy can burst through its restraint, Fisher uses it as an erotic device, heightening those areas (the chest, and the gently modelled underarm) that she finds arousing. The title also hints at the erotic nature of all confrontations between the artist and his or her model. By allowing himself to be drawn in such a touchingly vulnerable state, the model becomes (however temporarily) the artist's slave—the act of capturing his image is also one of erotic appropriation. At the same time, the cool tonalities of the image underline Fisher's detachment—light blue T-shirt, green cushions, even the slight pallor of the flesh, which almost suggests marble. The drawing remains carefully poised, a sensuous male nude handled in a classicizing spirit.

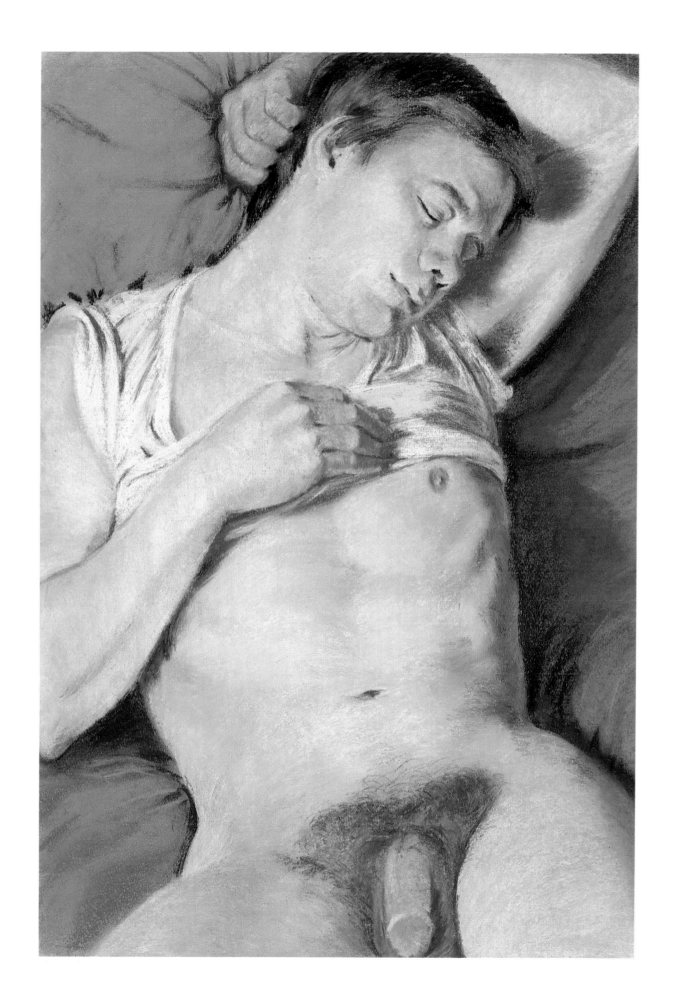

GENERAL BOOKS FOR FURTHER REFERENCE

Fuseli (exhibition catalogue, the Tate Gallery) London, 1975.

MELVILLE, ROBERT *Erotic Art of the West* London, 1973.

POSNER, D. *Watteau: A Lady at Her Toilet* London, 1973.

SCHIFF, GERT *The Amorous Illustrations of Thomas Rowlandson* New York, 1969.

SONTAG, SUSAN 'The Pornographic Imagination' in *Styles of Radical Will* London, 1969

WEBB, PETER *The Erotic Arts* (revised edn.) London, 1983.

WEBB, PETER and SHORT, ROBERT *Hans Bellmer* London, 1985.

ACKNOWLEDGEMENTS

Particular thanks, for helping with the research and choice of illustrations, are due to Sebastian Wormell; and also, for their help, to Sabine Tilly and Françoise Bertrand-Tilly. Victor Arwas, Christabel Briggs, Cavan Butler, Lynne Green, Allen Jones, Peter Webb, all generously assisted the author in the preparation of this book.

The works of Bellmer, Burra, Gorky, Hockney, Kirchner, de Kooning, Allen Jones, Kitaj are © 1986 the artist or their estates. The works of Grossman, Grosz, Picasso and Wesselman are © DACS, 1986.

1: Bildarchiv Preussischer Kulturbesitz, Berlin; fig. 1: Cambridge, Fitzwilliam Museum; 11: Courtesy of the Fogg Art Museum, Harvard University, Cambridge, Mass. Gift—Charles E. Dunlap; 9 (Charles Dering Collection), 23 (Mrs. Tiffany Blake), 26 (The John B. Wrenn Fund): © The Art Institute of Chicago; 20: Museum Ludwig, Köln; fig. 6: © Tomi Ungerer *Testament* (by courtesy of Jonathan Cape Ltd); 3, figs. 3, 7, 8: reproduced by Courtesy of the Trustees of the British Museum; 2, 25: © Christie's Colour Library; 29: © David Hockney, 1963; 31: Marlborough Fine Art; 32: Prudence Cummings; 4, 13, 28, fig. 5: Victoria and Albert Museum—Crown Copyright; 15: © Oslo Kommunes Kunstsamlinger—Munch Museet; 6: Ashmolean Museum, Oxford; 8: Cliché des Musées Nationaux, Paris; 12: Photo S.A.B.A.A., Paris; 14: Musée Rodin, Paris; 19: Cliché: Musées de la Ville de Paris; 30: The Art Museum, Princeton University. Museum purchase, the John Maclean Magie and Gertrude Magie Fund; 16: Graphische Sammlung Albertina, Vienna; 10: Gichner Foundation for Cultural Studies, Washington; fig. 4: Sterling and Francine Clark Art Institute, Williamstown, Mass.; fig. 2: Copyright reserved, reproduced by gracious permission of Her Majesty The Queen.